"I'm in a full-time relationship // with the w
is she ever. Her unsettling poems blaze acro
intelligence. The word "wild" is too tame to
or the pure panache. The poems sport with la
as they delve, refusing to settle for anything l   , sparking
synapses between thoughts. The "sign twirler"   dazzles throughout is so
wicked smart your head will spin. This is semiotics made flesh—full of color,
attitude, and kaleidoscopic, shifting embodiments. The twirler—like some
android-cyborg-posthuman being—can't be pinned down. Her subjectivity is
refracted in poems that fearlessly explore the contortions of received identities,
constructing a new erotics of science and philosophy along the way—an
innovative poetics with a sensibility so fresh it stuns. Raptosh's gorgeous strophes
have the effect of a mind-expanding drug, and the dazzle gradually darkens into
a surprising politics, a concern with privacy and surveillance. It would be hard
to overstate the brilliance of this boisterous, supercharged collection. Acerbic,
playful, and fiercely imagined, *Human Directional* is a book you'll read again
and again, enthralled by its inventive force and endless unfoldings.

—Alice Fulton, author of *Barely Composed*

Diane Raptosh is Whitman's heir apparent. Like Whitman, Raptosh's poetic
speakers contain multitudes, though instead of this self-amplification of identity
leading to more innate connection with others, Raptosh shows the complications
to intimacy that can arise when genders bend and change, animals morph into
other animals, selves disappear or blossom into others, and no boundary remains
stable. Raptosh's ecstatic, hilarious (and, yes, chaotic) multiplicity leads both to
confusion and an unquenchable longing in her speakers, where the self desires
coherence even as it recognizes such stability as improbability. Raptosh's poems
are a true postmodern romp, marrying Ovid with Tupac, prose with poetry, humor
with pathos, all while trying to construct—and deconstruct—the cohesive identity
that will allow one self to be truly intimate with another. Which direction does the
human go? In Raptosh's world, every which way: exuberantly, and at once.

—Paisley Rekdal, author of *Animal Eye*

Diane Raptosh's *Human Directional* points to all elements of the human
condition at once, but this is no scatter-shot. Every idea of which these poems
are comprised is surgical, exquisite; sure both of the emotional core from which
it sets out to explore, and the one it divines. From the collection's opening lines,
a Shakespearean roll call to the most fundamental essences of her audience,
Raptosh excites the heart's ability to feel what it doesn't know it can. This
first gathering and pointing is what sends us off to gorge ourselves on 'human
condition' and end up at all parts of the multiverse at once, thoroughly sated,
spectacularly amazed.

—Roger Bonair-Agard, author of *Bury My Clothes*

Once again, and never before, Raptosh hikes us deeper into the high hills of our own 'upside down' world. Book two of her brilliant unfolding trilogy illuminates the lush amber interior of her wonder; her swirling titles and jubilant magpie turns of phrase entreat. I was still 'touching my nose' long after my hand rested on the back cover.

—Nikky Finney, author of *Head Off & Split*

Diane Raptosh is one of the most exciting, inventive and remarkable poets writing today. If you haven't yet experienced her dynamic, eclectic mind, here is your chance.

—D.A. Powell, author of *Repast: Tea, Lunch, and Cocktails*

Nothing is off limits to the whirling speaker of Diane Raptosh's *Human Directional*, because "the space of// the thinkable is so much/ larger" than any one kind of poem, any form, any tone, can contain. So here are spidery couplets, blocks of off-kilter prose, Q&A as poetry, new compound words, fractions and factoids, whatever's necessary to speak the mind of this "every anyone," "a human tornado" whose careening meditations cover everything from Wittgenstein to "blue-footed-boobies" to "Gayle next door." But for all her pyrotechnics and sudden jerks and jumps, Raptosh is at heart an old-fashioned lyric poet, endearingly lonesome, hopeful about the prospect of a reader's company, generous with her ample wisdom and energy: "I am here," she writes, "because I have this tightness in my throat/ I don't want taking over the earth," and because "I fall slightly in love with whoever I get to/ stand next to." It's hard not to feel loved by these poems, and to love them.

—Craig Morgan Teicher, author of *Ambivalence and Other Conundrums*

"After reading Raptosh's tour de force, *American Amnesiac*, I wondered, what next? *Human Directional* is her answer—and it is a clear indication of Raptosh's infinite capacity to surprise. Subverting conventions and expectations, she is at once a poet, a philosopher, and an entertainer of an entirely new kind."

—Nin Andrews, author of *Why God Is a Woman*

Human Directional

ALSO BY DIANE RAPTOSH

Just West of Now (Guernica Editions, 1992)

Labor Songs (Guernica, 1999)

Parents from a Different Alphabet (Guernica, 2008)

American Amnesiac (Etruscan Press, 2013)

Human Directional

Diane Raptosh

etruscan press

Etruscan Press
Wilkes University
84 West South Street
Wilkes-Barre, PA 18766
(570) 408-4546

www.etruscanpress.org

Published 2016 by Etruscan Press
Printed in the United States of America
Cover design by L. Elizabeth Powers
Author photo by Eric Raptosh
Interior design and typesetting by Susan Leonard
The text of this book is set in Times New Roman.

First Edition

16 17 18 19 5 4 3 2 1

Library of Congress Cataloguing-in-Publication Data

Names: Raptosh, Diane, author.
Title: Human directional / Diane Raptosh.
Description: First edition. | Wilkes-Barre, PA : Etruscan Press, 2016.
Identifiers: LCCN 2015040468 | ISBN 9780990322160
Classification: LCC PS3568.A634 A6 2016 | DDC 811/.54--dc23
LC record available at http://lccn.loc.gov/2015040468

Please turn to the back of this book for a list of the sustaining funders
of Etruscan Press.

This book is printed on recycled, acid-free paper.

The world, which is upside down, will one day stand up straight.

—Eduardo Galeano

To Keats, Colette, and Greg

Heartfelt thanks go out to the following people for their generous assistance, friendship, and sustenance: Nin Andrews, Roger Bonair-Agard, Rob Carney, Deidre Chadderdon, Cassidy Clement, Keats Conley, Nikky Finney, Alice Fulton, Brandon Gubitosa, Greg Hampikian, Matthew Haynes, Dali Islam, Peter Jackson, Emily Leonick, Robin Lorentzen, Margento, Alan Minskoff, D.A. Powell, Colette Raptosh, Connie Raptosh, Eric Raptosh, Karen Raptosh, Paisley Rekdal, Carrie Seymour, Meg Simonton, Carla Stern, Craig Morgan Teicher, Katrin Tschirgi, and Lucinda Wong.

Special thanks to Phil Brady and Bill Schneider and all the fine people at Etruscan Press for their support of this book.

This Question is for Testing Whether You Are a Human Visitor

Would you rather marry a shoe

or eat a whole tub of butter?

Human Directional

Human Directional

I first-person triangular

Sign Twirler's Guide to the Multiverse

Indigenes, foundlings, sperm-persons
and egg-, chauffeurs, cabbies, teamsters,

cyborgs, lumpen silhouettes,
ladies and gentlemen of the jury

of my peers, and those of you
I think might like the *Yeah Yeah Yeahs*,

I am here because I have this tightness in my throat
I don't want taking over the earth.

To boot, I chose you
by discrete clues amidst the multitudes.

By faint directions. By sending out luteinizing hormones,
I want to noodge you into feeling

something vast. BTW, *a jury of one's peers:*
nowhere in the Constitution.

But it's a free country. So feel free
to interrupt. Already

your jawline's ease
says you will sway me

to be true about all things
from how to scour the consciousness of humankind

to how we'll find new tacks for striving to get by—
perhaps let soften our trapezii or reconstruct others'

inner soliloquies. I'm here now
to point and spin, to hang

deranging rectangles—sometimes-tiny plots—
intended to impact Earth and Mars

or tap unstudied spacecraft
but mostly to reach drivers of used cars, pedicabs

and townsfolk who haggle down the street.
Slow your vehicle to see: At 35

my pinkie and ring finger
got stuck curling down

as they would for a fist, like a country
that shall remain nameless.

This makes my left hand cluck
like a claw snared evermore in the symbol of peace.

Fair enough. I can still share with you my half
of the secret handshake, flash you

the Vulcan sign, then go on to perform the Wind-Up Toy
or Human Tornado—right at your feet—

and graze the flat of my palm
across your cheek to say good-bye.

If you have a little stubble
to scrape the anger of my teeth,

I can make it sound like we're munching
small apples *en masse*

or traipsing dirt lanes
totally in sync. More than anything,

I aim to untuck sound's omens,
hook up reason

with passion-acumen, see every scene
with the freak purity

of so many rattling pink eyes of riled albino deer.
Enlarge the flyspeck space

between each bone. If you can hear me,
touch your nose.

The Hidden Lives of Human Signs

I love signing *Twirler* on screens at the bank
        with only my index fingertip-pouf.

About the effect of membership
        in the tribe of people with single names,

I like it with love's detestation
        of most scripted things. *Love is*

a protein, I state to my selves
        and so doing, grow meatier,

showy as rosemary and garlic roast leg of lamb on a spit.
        If you don't believe me ask Virgil or Pink.

Ovid or 2pac. Pythagoras. Weegee.
        There's such a thing

as The Guild of One-Name Studies
        Centre of Excellence,

renowned for silken members' rooms.
        Do you believe in love? Madonna roars before she sings "Vogue."

As luck has it, I happen to have before me
        How to Read Wittgenstein,

written by someone named Monk. *How do you make love*
        last? I ask him, halfway through

the chapter "Picturing the World,"
        to which he rolls out:

                Play-acting—
                Singing catches—

                Making a joke; telling it—
                Solving a problem in simple arithmetic—

                Translating from one language into another—
                Asking, thanking, cursing, greeting, praying.

Shy men, this Monk, his Ludwig.
        Pure nonesuches! Still,

keen reader clan, I could really handle an assist from you:
        I want to learn to love things as they are

with the rapid startled unknowing
        of a floating dock washed up

on some far shore post-tsunami—vertigo-edged and dangling
        with only the most unheard of stripe of worm.

Did you hear the one about
        how Geronimo jumps from a plane and shouts, *"Meeeeeeeee!"*?

Does Plato count as having lived mononymously?
        Scheherazade, yes. Lassie?

Do porn stars count?
        Is it plain odious that I love

the way mule deer move
        their ears almost constantly

as much as I love anyone on earth?
        If it is, don't tell me.

If it isn't too.

Sign Twirler Stands Like Michelangelo's Man in a Circle

I was just standing here   thinking of space junk
when suddenly   I saw myself looking
down at my limbs   as if from afar —

loose and precise   as a sketch
of an exploded   lawnmower.   It made me feel
bloomed.   Barbed.   Roomier.

I do!   Hate.   How a given system for living
strong-arms its way into being
the only possible one.   I'd like to burn

the words   *quench   douse   extinguish.*
Listen. I contain too many people to try
and be true to any singleton.

Remorse of course breaks down
to *bite again.*   I therefore want
to date the human version of a sprife

since it can shiv veal,   fork
a quarter of pumpkin mousse pie
and scoop bouillabaisse without a glitch   almost all

at the same time   *Rest Unrest*   Precisely what I'd like
to do with my live Three-in-One,
whom I'll call *Herm*—   his and her

hands lethal as hooves:
lettuce fetishist   yes. *He-She-It* must scarf purple corn,
lashes long as gouges in a text.   Love with me   if you will

those roving flecks of paint
and dust,   each star-crossed spacecraft,   rocket
motor effluents.   That dwarf minor planet *Makemake.*   Permanency,

Herm,   is punishment—the human face   in its turn
so hush-hush   it's a shame we have to wear it out
for all to view.   For this reason

let us listen   to each other
only   through the halls of our backs || looking opposite
ways.   We'll baste dark calms   in Volcano electronic cigarettes.

Digital Billboard with Fidgeting Images

We have the same number of hairs on our skin
          as chimpanzees, just that ours
have grown useless. This helps us to

                sweat more easily, make life harder
                for ticks—our forebears clearly

    semi-aquatic, dipping finned toes in
the swimming pool of the self
        in its maiden phase. I sometimes feel

    electric ants scuttle up my arms and legs—
the restlessness, perhaps,

                of *Thetys vagina* salps

                              which locomote by

        pumping raw sea through
            gelatinous bodies. The yellow-orange-faced

    Columbian katydid sports ears like an old person's
only it stows them inside the crooks
      of their knees. I'd scratched

  this into my *Square Deal*.   Dung beetle. First ever creature

      to read the light of the Milky Way
          to chart its own path. The atoms

             that make up who we think ourselves to be:
             mostly empty space.

                      Ah cigarette—   singlehanded
                    strong emotions surrogate!

    I'm pretty sure
          such busyness lays the base for laziness,

wee gob of phlegm
in every apothegm.

Of Genders and Genres

It is frequently said that *he, she,* or *it* is really a *piece of work.*

Interspace

Her boyfriend just admitted he has a hetero-man crush on Andrew Bird, whose first violin was a Cracker Jack box—a ruler taped to it—and this makes her want to swat him with a three-inch-thick stick and take him down now. She wants to swim smack into him: melon-scent, lake shaft, mud-suck. She wants him to fever her while he craves Bird, to hymn his own thickness—granitic and oozy— into the lax pink architecture of her inner city and stick there, summing up space and time while now and then he loops through one of her slick underground corridors back to the concert, pausing to smooch nut and neck on Andrew's guitar or to kvetch with Bird's early Suzuki teacher and quietly bow. She wants him to whistle while he works Bird-yen and her, man-moving and mons-alert, glockenspiel thumping light hammers at the foot of the bed, tri-colored herons and gray tailed grackles swooshing in and out of their bivouac, their layer cake of slurp and plume, horsehair and hip jab: pure osseousness. This is how knowing is—springing things into the light, this is how *rev* issues into *elation;* this, how flock-love spins roots and lilacs forth.

Husband

She didn't have one, and never had, if *have* was the right verb for knowing someone in this way and referring to someone with this word. She had had children. Two of them. She had had friends. She had had, or, as she had heard it said, had *taken* lovers. Still, through all these years she had felt more or less tended to, almost thoroughly husbanded, though by what or whom exactly it was hard to say—certainly by some of the men she had been with, and some of the women, sometimes by her own mother even, but equally often by a single idea, such as Schoenberg's, who believed all progress in social thinking and feeling had come about through force of longing. With equal frequency, though with less predictability, she had felt cared for by certain objects: a spotted yellow pear, the dark fetal curl of the dog's tail, that ancient hay derrick, tall and rangy, pointing out the far end of the world. Sometimes when she went to a movie by herself—something she often did—she'd tell the ticket-taker that her husband would arrive at any minute. She simply liked the sound of the word, and she took it entirely, and many times a day, as hers.

Traffic Circle

Here is my sister, steady as a table, and this woman with whom she shares a
meal of eggplant and snow peas is my mom. For years, they have dined nightly
like this. When my sister goes quiet, as she does tonight, green eyes staring like
grapes, she is my father, and I become the youngest in the house, never mind
the presence of my teen-aged nephew and my tiny daughter building towers of
quarters together on the floor. In such times, my sister's son turns into my brother,
and thereby, my children's uncle. My own brother, by his own admission, not to
mention our mom's, insists he and my sister should long ago have traded loins.
For a few years in the seventies, after our father died, he and I were, respectively,
our mother's mom and dad. Because time is one fierce wheel sprung from the
trunk of a single bristlecone pine, back then I was simultaneously my mother's
dad, my sister's child, and my nephew's sibling, even though he was decades
from having been born, while my full-grown father was from day one the not-
quite-son I never had. My smallest daughter behaves in a manner *grandmotherly*.
My oldest daughter, taller than I, wants to have a family bash honoring the hunch
she is more or less a happily gay man swathed in an almost-woman's body.
On her eighteenth birthday—with only her boyfriend as witness—she wants to
change her first name to *Merganser.*

The Three-Body Problem

Solutions to the three-body problem may be of an arbitrary complexity and are very far from being completely understood. –Scholar*pedia*

i) Periodic Systems of Astronomical Interest

Like some Carica papayas, George Washington had the XXY condition. He pointed out that he was statuesque, had no kids but rather broad hips, a size 13 boot, and a fondness for swatches of calico. He liked to rub and compare them, to watch them through moon-mote, to flutter and twirl them in horseshoe orbits. He powdered his red-brown hair and tied it in a braid down his back like a small mane. When George was elected, a czarina reigned in Russia, a shogun in Japan. Only the office of President endures. In this case we can ignore the influence of the light body on the other spheres. For assurance, Washington carried a pocket sundial wherever he went. He bred hound dogs he named Tarter, True Love, and Sweet Lips. He would spell words like *blue* as *blew, oil* as *oyl,* and *eie* for an *eye.* The six white horses in Washington's stables had their teeth brushed every morning. Washington's orders. As can be seen, the three-body problem—its four degrees of freedom—offers myriad options for public service.

ii) Without Loss of Generality, We Consider the Three-Body Problem on a Plane

Three healthy male volunteers in their 20s were placed bare-chested in front of cameras in light-tight rooms for 20 minutes every three hours from 10 a.m. to 10 p.m. for three days. Researchers watched body-gleam spool through the dark. "If you see the sheen from the surface of three bodies, you can see the whole body condition," states researcher Etsuko Kobayashi from Kyoto U.

iii) Three Bodies of Equal Mass Follow Each Other at Uniform Spacing

If there was a drowning in the River Rappahannock, her mother would

note how that was the third in a series, even if it was not, or how there

would be a third drowning if two had taken place within the past six years.

iv) <u>Celestial Mechanics</u>

Her boyfriend is the mother of her child.

v) <u>Two Bodies Move Closely Round Each Other and Around a Third Body Far Away</u>

The oil-black aril-covered seeds in the papaya's core, which smack
of nasturtiums, have contraceptive effects on adult male langur monkeys

and handpicked blue-green eyed persons . . . .

Your Attention, Please

The first jawed fish, *Microbrachius dicki,* performed the planet's debut sex 385 million years ago. On the male specimens of *M. dicki,* scientists found bony structures splayed on each side of the fish, etched with a groove to deliver the sperm. On females, spiny genital plates gripped the male in place, Velcro-like.

Each looked like a computer mouse with fins.

"They couldn't have done it in missionary position," says paleontologist J. Long, Flinders University, Adelaide, Australia. The first ever sex was sideways—a *do-si-do.* The moon on Earth's limb: that spin.

They've re-tapped copulation's origins: Early jawed vertebrates. From them, the cartilaginous. Their descendants. Us.

• •

Reader. Have you ever been that grievously unmade?

Rugged Western Individualism

A man who is his own wife gives birth to his identical twin through his belly button. For months, he thinks it's a cyst. A fistula. An ingrown hair. A fir tree germinating in his spleen. He father-mothers this shriven boy, fine and tiny as walnut lung. With equal parts sweetmeats and a firm touch, he bathes this baby in a small green bowl—that wee, webbed blood of living kin. Nights, the man daubs his chafed nipples with tea bags, lays a wet cloth on his eyes. He tugs at the far left swirl of his mustache. He sometimes wonders aloud: *Am I famished? Is this fullness?* When he kisses his left hand, his wife strokes his cheek.

At the Symposium on the Necessity of Beauty

It was, she was certain, bigamy: being here with her husband.

Enter the Kingdom

Bok choy boy, fiddlehead—we don't call each other vegetables half often enough.
Begin begging me to, spiny earth-culled cardoon, parsnip-kin, pet pea: O sweet
erect jambu, meaty edamame, let us roll our strength into a cabbage globe, let
us tear pleasure with loosestrife, with carrot blades swooped in fluted pumpkin.
Fust not, svelte luffa, endive of my eye: Let's let our vegetable love fatten like
empires—at mudspeed. But more slow. Be partially mine, sweet Swiss chard, flea
beetle-bitten arugula: Let us gnash our teeth in up-and-down rows, let me scrape
your green meat, swill divisible hairs, Jerusalem artichoke, oh, sunroot and earth
apple. Kale spine. Gherkin. Malabar gourd. Ah, sunflower! Flung beet, stout red
hen, let me eat the mother in you.

Garden Variety Glide

Snail one, whom we will call She/he, finishes starting off sex by shooting the dart first. She/he does unto/undoes—or tries to—Snail two, while he/she tries sticking in her/him tiny silver harpoons sheathed in thick goo: This after intense pressure's collected in the blood sinus. This after they've circled each other for up to six hours, sexes swelling the backs of their necks. Next they mesh tentacles, nosh along lips and genitals. Snail two might flub his and her shot half of the time, botching the launch so the spike bounces off. Snail one might make the barb miss her or his partner entirely, for simply the feel of pure air. A Japanese breed might stab his and her partner 3,000 times in one pursuit—flanges and gels fluorescing, lance-work fed by vibration of stamen and pistil: Light of the wooer's eye, and pursuer to a slightly lesser degree her- and himself, at last so thoroughly love-bulleted, Samurai Boygirl figures he and she will call it good, gliding into the blur on a film of white mucus.

Junction

She thought of herself as an old man, even a wise one, which is why she wanted
to move to this neighborhood of old folks in the first place—the grass not her
job to green up, the weeds not her chore to burn down. As an old man, she
saw as her main task learning to die, which meant, in the words of Montaigne,
unlearning how to be a slave—her daily thoughts, creatures of edges like so
many tottering polar bears. Being an old man also made it hard to be a young
man's wife. The old man blushed on her forearms when her husband came home
from work. Sure enough, some nights the old man liked to look up the crooked
spiral skirts of yellow larches—his favored way to unwind before the day's last
meal. Her husband often wondered out loud *What gives?* And *Why do I always
have to repeat myself so many times?* Not to mention their twins, who liked
to jump double-dutch rope from smack inside the old man's skull. They drank
almost nothing their first two years but old-man teat, whose vestige of kindness
they'll never come to forgive.

The Inner Coat

A couple takes their Akita to the vet. The woman speaks of her husband:
A lineman. Sets up shop in the air. She blurts terms like *bull pen* and *spud
wrench. Skinner* and *baloney bender.* The husband weeps smiles. She turns
to the dog. She goes on about the dog's inner coat, his small heart. The bloat.
His catlike feet. Teeth that meet in a scissors. The dog lies down, head on the
woman's toes. *Oh I'm so tired,* the woman lilts. *I just have to lie down here.*
The vet looms like a stranger too familiar to know. The husband cocks his head
as the dog has his nails trimmed. *My, what strong black nails I have,* the woman
squeaks. She palms the dog's head. She stares into his round three-cornered
eyes, scratching her forearm with her eyeteeth.

Ballroom-Dance with a Sign in Order to Point It in the Right Direction

A small sea moves off the breeze,
a thousand crude leaf rafts trekking aloft.
Ah, thirst for air does look like verse—
the sounds of each word
breathing clear of its meaning.

This thought makes reason stare:
The timbre of, let's say, *aubergine*
practically fracks you with feminine niff.

What's more, I'm embarrassed
to say *bruschetta* out loud,
so I couldn't make it

to Lizbeth's costume party last week.
Do you pronounce the crackling
in the middle of that piece of bread
or say it *shh*? Absurdity
is a luxury sure as money

causes dearth, and I'm still here
using signs like guitars with a mind
to feed people what they can feel.

When did you last
fix your lips in a kiss
to whistle like a traffic guard?

Curb your car. To really live
there should be dread too.
Therefore, I shall try, under sun's gaze
and through lesser fire
to arrive at being

more amply with others,
as though from underneath. Elm root.
Kelp frond. Sea squirt complex

as we are: walker, laggard, trucker.
Sprinter—can near air weather your joy
like troupes of finned wizards?

Sign Twirler Balances Six Rectangles at Once

Something's so right   about the sounds in   *diatomaceous earth*
that to speak the words   aloud alone   to the day   automatically
slips you into   chiropractic alignment,   brews you
vivid as   boybird,   grand as a bat   making mental   maps   on the fly.
Did you ever doubt   you were even really human?   Have you

ever felt   you were at the same time   every   living   thing?
The roof of your mouth   is a swank   planetarium,
and elephants croon much as we   at very low frequencies.
Plants know when the insects eat,   while corals release   their eggs
in such synchrony   you can almost begin   to smell all beings

you've   lost in layers   like a blind dog.   Have you
ever sat   and watched a boom   just hang there   from a
hay rig's apex? Did you ever sense   you had a hair   angling off
your sternum that was never there?   And while we are here,
which   possible world   do you think will rip a dawn   plumb

into Earth's prime artery?   Columbus may have set off   a chain
of events   that cooled Europe's climate,   which means unpeopling
a place can spawn a whole Ice Age. *Hew!* They shut off people's water
in Detroit,   which goes   to show the state of the meek.   Mad
world needs some justness dusted off. A beauty rucksack. Deduction

has it   history has opened   for suggestions   and I can
hear you all too coolly thinking straight into me—spine   in its undulant
plain line, full sun   halfway through   its energy-producing life.
The air is madcap-hot   and hilly. I'm standing here   near bags
of powdered hard-shelled algae; my shepherd Toby chases his tail~~

a neurosis call *whirling.*   Get it: Every manner of bot   can
groove. What if the womb's griot   found a way to   hand you
straight back   to yourself,   stripped   of all status
and code   —tell the slant   /
but do so truly :   Would you have any idea   what to do with you?

II the way to green air

Views from a Former Contortionist

She missed looking at mountains and seeing men in them, tens of them maybe—rows of rough-hewn torsos waiting for her to finally knuckle down. She wanted still to feel the need to mount them, one at a time, to lay to, to undo their detachment, to back-stride every set of jags on the Cascades, to hasp onto the furthest peaks of the Brabazon Range and fall to work, one quick pump of every other point on the Carpathians, whip hand not hanging on to anything. She missed the need to think she had to do something swashy or wry with her tongue on the west tip of the Rockies—bent up and scarp-faced, to lick out the fusty, unseen rucks of so many folding contortionists, or, to do something more rose-hued, like bleed all over the pointiest part of Los Cuernos del Paine in southern Chile or ease slowly down the nose of each face in the Presidential Range. She yearned to long again for the mass of the great great Grampians in Oceania lying in wait beneath her, for the Slovene Karavanke chain to openly slake her liquid need. Not to mention effects of thinking of the Montes Recti and Mons Hansteen—mountains on the moon—ready for just such scenes to come to fruition. Nor to mention Cuba's Sierra Maestra: She'd always wanted to hover just over that mother-idea.

Materfamilias **Leaflet**

Mothers among African black eagles hoard loads of rock hyrax carcasses—jackrabbit-sized mammals that hide in the kopjes—yet feed just one of two eaglets. Moms stand by looking bored as A-chick jabs its sib to bits. Great egret babes fight to the death. Motherbird yawns. Same with pelicans, cranes, and blue-footed boobies. Fatal battles brim in hyena and fox dens, ditches seething with cannibal tadpoles. Some mother hawks and owls halve their broods and eat them too. As for that panda-ma, did she not give birth to twins? Magellanic penguin moms lay two eggs and let one starve. Deep in the forest a black stork that's fed her nest a bolus of chewed fish grabs the smallest heir by the head and chucks it over the nest-rim. Fatal eviction. Rhesus monkey moms kick, bite, hit, and gash their tots as regular diet. Most mother squids lay eggs on ocean floors and scram. Ocean sunfish flee three hundred million fecundated eggs in one-shot spawns. Rodent mums might quaff their sickliest to spare the rest. To transgress their way into safety, mothers among monkeys, mice, and lions ditch newborns when new males swash into view. Pregnant female mice that spot the new guy sometimes just abort their young. Same with wild mustang moms, a phenom called the *Bruce effect.* The neighbor's guinea hen will trot so fast her brood can't possibly keep up. A famished lactating chimp will slay and gulp a groupmate's kid grief-free: a swift meal. A mouthfeel. A lean mound of lipids. The mother nurse shark boasts two uteri but lacks placentae: Feeds her inner fish on skins and fins of fellows in the womb. Among ants of a rare genus, tired queens will, of an evening, kick up their feet, chew holes in their larvae and chug their issue's ooze.

Take this, each of you, and sip. And feast.

From Staple to Symbol

In the name of the annual yam festival, gangs of Trobriand Island women
and girls—breasts coconut-oiled, pollen-cloaked, red palm bands wound in
their hair—pounce on a man from a different clan when he's in the gardens,
haul him beneath clumps of dried banana leaves, past rows of thatched huts
strung with tubers in baskets, and cast him into a limestone cave where they
proceed to rape him. Toddlers rock yams in crooks of arms; men in schoolgirl
pairs flee for days—fear nicking their skin, guava-smell quavering out and in
with the Solomon Sea whose slurry flops its volute swarms of whelks and flint
chips: jellyfish as jut and pulse of abdomen, underswells churning coquinas,
sunrays and slippery frills. The village chief consents to all this: yam risen from
staple to symbol, its very root flung from the Wolof verb "eat," making—or
wreaking—love reckoned able to cede their crops' meaty fertility. When the
ravishing's done (to marry, one need merely stay in bed with a man until dawn),
woman or girl nips the man's eyebrows off. Or a batch of his lashes. Letting
him go, she plucks from the sand her *katububula,* garland of white frangipani
blooms, petals tugged back with spider web strands to loosen the weft and reel
of milk. With frenzied delicacy. Sucking out eyebrow hairs from between
her front teeth.

Motherhood as Momentary Characteristic

Perhaps she is not so strange in the final analysis, though she sleeps with a
bandit mask on and red rubber bullets wedged in her ears, which she holds
in place with a kerchief until well within her office, where she shreds striped
documents and sends down forms in outsized envelopes—shining and steadfast
as mystic galoshes—sometimes from the eleventh floor to a city far from the
state in which she shares a beige townhouse on a wind-blown dune with this
tribe of unquiet natives, the plumes on whose heads have yet even to reach
the base of her coccyx.

Intersectional

Linda has been dating Glenn, and doing so, often hits on the side of him who is his mom, Janette, who wears red oblong sunglasses inside and at night. Glenn, beginning to love Linda, falls mostly for the region in her that is her father, Stan, who underlies his daughter's every move. Who ceded her his woodsmoke voice. His forehead scrim. His stoicism. Glenn's deceased dad, Will, a quiet man who forged himself a long-term home across his son's alleles, is smitten by Stan too. Linda's mom, Maureen, enters in this bond by stealth: a point in the air, a twitching of Linda's ears, a tune interstitial, which only Glenn can hear. When Will, who likes to hide along the left side of Glenn's chest, tries to dote on Maureen—to bring her some oolong tea with traces of blueberry, or plump the fat green pillows cupping her feet, Janette tenses her jaw and pecks at her glasses. Stan thins his eyes to teeny horizons. Linda and Glenn, dazed by they haven't the vaguest what, skulk around the room wondering if it's time to finally start seeing other people.

Ghost Sign

When they fight in sign language, you can hear the skin of their thumbs slough.

Broadsheet from the Family Bed

Great Aunt Josephine and Uncle Vince stretch and shift. Arranged in fan shape
at the mom's right hip are all the men she's ever been with, washed in by the
years. The youngest daughter, eyes wide beneath closed lids, has three fathers:
the mother's ex—whose eyebrows twitch as he blinks off a dream—and the
mom's current husband as stepdad; the youngest girl's birth father and mom hail
from the northeast lip of Nanjing city. They lie here every night, quiet as air,
one of their hands gripping the mattress rim, another hand fluting the skin on the
waters of Xuanwu Lake, near the foot of the far blue bed of Mount Jiuhua.

Scrolling Light Box with the 12 O'Clock News

Women start out happier than men but die sadder, claims a praised scientist. Men begin more unhappily yet by age forty-eight or –nine begin to match women in gladness. Economics Professor Paul F— settles happiness' cash values thus: Marriage is worth $28,724.57 to men and $14,181.75 to women. The birth of a child: $24,641.38 to a man and $7,910.43 to a woman. A divorce: $8,088.95 (loss) to a woman and $99,328.97 (loss) to a man. The death of a loved one: $118,975.53 to a woman and $570,200.24 to a man (not the value of life lost but of life left). Illness: $45,710.58 (loss) to a woman and $327,113.02 (loss) to a man. Finally, moving to a new house marks a $2,367.34 gain to a woman but makes men shout like Earth heard from space ($14,534.60 loss). Professor F—, of Queensland University of Technology, was earlier this year named best Australian economist under age 40.

Sign Twirler Crunches Some Numbers

Dealing in numbers might halt the mind's
stalking more solemn things:

Willie Nelson wrote "Crazy"
in 20 minutes. Figure.

It takes 13 million calories
to raise a child. Measure twice;

cut once. *Triskaideka-*
phobia is the word for fear

of the number 13,
whose microbe I carry.

Global average temps have risen by 1.6 degrees
since the start of the 20th century.

Seventy percent of the world's umbrellas
are made in China. The average daily charge

for an electric vehicle
is less than one dollar. The mayor

of Whoville
had 96 daughters. Thirty-three thousand

asteroids and 20 new comets are aiming their whims
straight at Earth. *Pseudopseudohypoparathyroidism,*

much more fun to say
than come down with,

marks my lucky number, 12,
through strict syllable count.

Over the seven days
between March 27 and April 3,

28 people were killed
by U.S. police.

Everyone must be safe
for us all to be so. The One

brings the many out of itself, Goethe was fond
of avouching. But what happens in those heights

a half-hand's breadth past the universe's edge? And what,
for all the world, might be the term for dread over that?

What word so lovely and lonesome, so truehearted—blue-white spark so lithely out of control
it finally brings full opening to the groin?

Step on a Crack, You Break

The matter before us is my mother.
Her mind, embryo pendant in water.

    The slope of the riverbank
    we used to maunder. Among

        some things the body can't remember:
        Matter and *mother* burst from the baby-talk

    ma, which suckle-uproar also birthed
    metropolis. Bridgehead and truss. The flat-

topped ziggurats. *Matter,* O mighty cloth.
Mom, the hard timber used within carpentry.

    Mama as groundmass and muck.
    Materiel and cereal crop. . . . This is

        the farmer sowing her corn that worried
            the cat that lay in the house.   This is the line

    that helps keeps things level.   Listen, Ma, I am
skittering out of my head—

        a human tornado

            dervishing off the chink of Earth's curb

Ours is the Age of Pre-Post-Hope

Tonight's the night to spin a world
that does not reproduce the now,

like the inventor of the Vegetebrella,
who thought the beauty of the simulacrum

of a butter lettuce head
and levered silver pole could live as one.

This Kindle is jealous
of that dulcimer, and even these specks

of tension make me feel
rag-edged as a contorted filbert.

Consider, if you will, the following:
Cities should try to sell umbrellas

only in slim numbers,
forcing strangers in twos

to rub arm hairs together.
Padmasambhava is said to have said

the basis for realizing enlightenment
is the human body. Understand.

These pairs of persons
wouldn't even have to talk,

looking over each other's shoulders
at the town's shins—

broad umbel shadowing
the earth between them,

carving raw closeness
with the lights of their ribs.

Human Arrow with Necks of Trilliums

after Neruda

I want to ask you to walk with me
toward no movement and not

saying a word   I want to
see if we can cover hard ground

like mule deer on tiptoe
ears pricked against far

dry heat   I want to know
if we can arrive

not quite in a clearing
purfled with sage and bitterbrush

I want to see if we can
approach not coming to

terms, no goods
to chaffer over—half

a dozen headless trilliums pointing the way
to green air   I want

to go with you to watch
the daily blades of light

layer that dun-brown butte just out
our back door   I will acquire

your quiet   And tender
you mine with this proviso:

that we shape the print of
our silence   so

we do not have to   ever
fathom one another

Direction Versus Bearing

I fall slightly in love with whoever I get to
stand next to. With beauty's hypotheses.
With you I address. And then there's this:
I'm having an affair with truth.

This sheathes me in alpenglow.
Razor burn. Should I choose a woman
or man for the lifelong? Is there such a thing
as the thought of a feeling? Regardless of status

everyone's secretly married
to somebody else, to patterns
of small things' reticent densities: packs
of filter-free cigarettes, those wee submarines

of jellyfish grubs,
the means by which spider blood
fluoresces under UV lights.
I contain pulchritude, yes.

A-choo! I was born. Perhaps I am
too much my mother and father—
more niche than genre,
more poncho than program. Marriage

should be made illegal for everyone, replaced
with two-year contracts
like those for the tiny thumb pianos
we use to text our friends:

Hey girl,
have you ever had mule deer
leave their heart-shaped tiptoe prints
on your side lawn?

Poster in the Present Perfect Continuous Negative Tense

You have never been staying home enough lately

• • •

The basenji hasn't been yodeling since you've been gone

• • •

I haven't been *folding up my end of the stick,* Granddad says

• • •

I haven't been hitting anyone on the back with my cleats

• • •

You have never been staying home enough lately

• • •

I haven't been telling many lies   I haven't been getting too sick

• • •

What's in our water bottles has not been tasting like water

• • •

Granddad's breath hasn't exactly been smelling like kiwi fruit

• • •

You have always not been coming home when I need you to

Light Wind Lifts Language's Dress Up

July sky files another joy, and I'm out hanging laundry
on the lowest branches of our honey locust.

It's Friday. It is,
as the kids say, *hella hot,*

and as I lay damp socks across
the longest seedpods, I am put in mind

of Wong Bock Sing, who at 67
took in bundles of wash,

labored over tub and ironing board,
then delivered his completed works

to local clients—without complaint
roundabout 1913,

which reminds me of the eternal
neverness of now

and the girl
with the Justin Bieber haircut

I met in Rhodes Skate Park,
who prattled on about the honeycombs of Chinese tunnels

she's sure must roam the undersides
of Boise. Legend's residue, yes—

a work we might dub *tall nonfiction.*
O hungry readership, do you believe

it's against the CC&Rs to dangle Shock Sock river shoes atop
the neighbor's curb to dry? Did I remember to return two eggs

to Gayle next door? Those wine glasses to Peter and Eric?
We live in the land of the Shoshone and Bannock.

Shouldn't I already have been always kinder,
more openhanded—a titch

more alert?
O humid river shoe, to be

means not to know entirely how to,
though if you could look around, you'd see that

while the din rages
elsewhere about Islam,

a new mosque, painted eggshell and green,
opened its quiet doors

on Cloverdale, welcoming Bosniaks.
Anyone can come.

It is here, in what one Kosovar called *Potato City,*
we got these folk beliefs:

If you see a blue jay on Friday,
you will have good luck,

and *Thick slices of bread*
are called "step-mother slices."

It is here, where of a summer's night
you might go out to hear the band Amuma Says No,

the accordion saying *yes, yes, yes* the whole while,
saying *Sí, se puede,*

saying *Hal luuqad marna kuma filna,* Somali
for *one language is never enough,*

saying, *Halleuliah, Homeslice:*
This is a good use of our life.

We Need a Case for Doing Good in Minute Particulars

But take for instance the worm. Neither its five aortic arches,
which ease would call *hearts,* nor even its six historic
spellings, *wyrme, wirm, wrim, wrm, wurm, wormr,* warmed
her to it, howsoever. *Hosowevre. Whevoroes. Wosohever.*

Clean Garage *Rag*

The sheen of its floor she finds garish. And doesn't the room preserve certain rage, so many objects aging in there? That pair of *rags* flung forward and back—the noun and verb bunched up in *garage*. In that word is almost *garbage* itself. Gobs of popped balloon and chicken legs cleave in the bin behind the overhead door, waiting to be trucked to the dump, shoehorned into crypts. Refuse preserved into perpetuity. A village can mature for years in history's cask: *Garage* sounded too much to her like the town *Goražde*, which tanks and bullets almost blurred into a grave. Sometimes a sole American house will take a back seat to four garage doors aimed at the street like linked, discrete front lines. Maybe a clean garage helps people feel saved, every extra roof tile in its place, cat box liners quiet beside the anti-freeze. Almost any American garage is *car lodge*. Perhaps behind one of those doors lies an hygienic fix-it shop in which someone wears an oil-stained monkey suit and goggles at a lathe. But doesn't a clean garage finally mean *too much time on the hands?* Let such a one lean in to sop landfill ooze finding its blind way to groundwater. *Rag, rag, rag,* she thinks to herself. Better a keen barrage of kindness, an idea's clear lingering, a quick bite of ling cod at the first plink of dawn.

Fire Sign

Each July, long after the hills have been shorn, a man on our street runs from his house—robe flapping its arms, dog off its leash. He yells out "Fire, fire," and "Help me, help please." His dog, a Basenji, screams. One of us springs to them, summoning calm. We're sure no one's in flames; the wife is long gone. The dog cries provable tears. Yet we realize none of us has not been stirred at some point to do what he's done, or something in a similar vein, though in each instance it has taken every speck of grit, plus the will of beasts and ancestors, to almost thoroughly shush us.

III ninety-degree angle to the chest

The Hope of Sound

Here we have another day
to remind us
there will come a day
another one won't come.

My alphabet's full
of lawnmower fumes,
Life out shining its bike,
and I would like a dress of water

pinned to me,
shoulder blades agleam
near the back darts,
the unseen blurbed to this world

by the seen.
Even Zennists with clear eyes
cannot save themselves pointblank.
I walk in tightly packaged ways

yet know to enlarge the breath's world
beyond the scrim
of asphalt, stoplight,
intersection.

You might say I'm already living
a little on the afterside,
and Toby respects me enough
to think me one of him. What's more,

I've always already been spoken for
by crossing zones. By the hope of sounds. It might be a stretch
to say you'd believe in the ghostliest hums
as a means of retreading the world.

So think of your favorite civic adjectives.
Together, we'll begin to draft
a better system in scratchitti
on the sides of buses. The tools to do this:

Pennies.
Keys.
Pumice stone.
Lava rock.

Screwdriver.
Box cutter.
Exacto knife.
Drill bit:

Receptive ~~ benevolent ~~ tolerant ~~ unchained

~~ Likes to flirt with angers on the train

Fifth and State

Toby blindly half-sits at my heels:
        a canine bird marking out the sky.

I'm on my corner, holding a sign
        that says *Title Loans.* Springsteen

yowls in my earbuds,
        the world's dogsbody.

I'm sure now I'm really going to miss the world
        when my day comes, despite

our military chiefs white-hot
        for war over the Arctic Circle.

I'm a sign-carrying member
        of the breed who stands

to fail at living.
        Perhaps when each of us grows up

we'll settle all our scores with Earth,
        and this is hard to put

in no uncertain terms.
        Do you suppose that nonstop sense

of almost fraudulence
        might be honesty at its most purebred?

I'm halfway in
        a deep *amour* with you.

That's what you might call
        a *superovershare,* but this could be to a *T*

what the great seedpod we're walking on
        needs. *None of this*

means a shooting war is likely
        at the North Pole any time soon, assures the AP,

so relax your stance, twirl freely.

  O darlin' Billy, O pedestrian, biker, oh whoever draws

near, I give to you

   a full-on blank page—that doctrine of softness.

That fiefdom.

   Draft your superovershare within:

Experiment on Backs of Soup Labels

It takes 70 muscles   to mouth a single word.
Sometimes I wish   I could
have been the Queen   of Jazz
since scat lets you skirt

actual thought.   Some months past
lacking an S.O.   I sang "A Fine Romance"
to a cinnamon roll.   An autumn blaze maple.
A thank you-based god,

slap-happy as a jellyfish's oral arms.
Follow. Unfollow.   Yesterday I decided to
take the word *rapture*   back
from its   religious captors

so I scrawled it   in black ink
on the glue side   of a soup label
and scorched it   with a Strike-Anywhere.
I wanted to   let the word recatch

the quilled swoop   and swift
loose-jointed lift   of the African secretary bird,
part eagle   part crane—
lank but queenlike.   Set | |

reset.   Part of the ongoing work.
I wanted to retune *rapture*   to try to mean something
like *civic overjoy*   forged
from a mini-model   of a world

I hadn't yet seen.   Time to
lower the ceiling   for feeling things.
To name   a comfort commission.
To free the drunken moose from that apple tree.

[ ] Is a Sign That Means *Hug for the Horse Forequarters of the Hippocampus*

Take it. Sometimes you have to
close your mouth

to keep the heat inside,
but I am in the mood

for verb: *Quiet* and *wolf* are a pair
of my favorite cross-dressers.

Life is too short to eat
what's in you: Heart cells

titivate and renew
in time—thanks

to small molecules rousing them to.
Men have come

and gone, empires
tanked, but mites

have hardly changed.
And might not

one's separate quiet
dust up something like decency?

This world is gravid
with better lode, the way

that crack in Africa may coin
a new sea, the way beetles are born

in a nougat of mother-muck
and then carry armored suits

made of the stuff, brindled
as magnified sand. Thinking thinks it's aided

by the shoulders'
sloping closer

to the brain. And now
that word *shoulder*

wants to turn
suddenly strange: *ou* grim humerus,

dread's knapsack,
florid hump-backed fly—

Is there anybody there?

True Life is Lived When Tiny Changes Occur, Says Tolstoy

Male fleas boast backwards-
pointing body hairs,

short spines athwart
their frames and flanked bouquet

of blushing genitalia—fifty names to sketch their makeup:
Tergites. Sternites. Apodemes.

The *Palliolum of the Aedeagus*—however you say that,
his *House of Phallus:*

two penises measuring a third of his full length, plus
sensory suckers braced atop his eyes,

which he uses to shift
his girl more or

less liturgically in space
for copulation

from beneath. He can do this
almost as soon

as he quits
the cocoon.

         Every time the jaw drops

            a syllable is born.

Art Must be Useful to the People

Summers, school-age Tolstoy held the densest book he could find
at a ninety-degree angle to his chest—six minutes each day—
getting his forearms fit for sorrow.

A Sign Said *There Are 16 Million Eyes in the City*

The sun is out taking selfies
in blue-brown puddles
edging my street.   Which for some reason

makes me think   of that sentence
on the poster   I saw last year
on the train in Manhattan

trademarked   by Homeland Security:
   If you see something,
   say something.

I saw it
also at the state fair.
                          In the meantime
we stand here together, sidewalk and I,
until only the ether remains.

And I will get back—
               maybe
to how   *unsubtling*   it is
that a sentence   could be thought
   made   of such stuff

as might be   government-trained
to turn us   all in
to each other's informants,

much the same way
whales' layered earwax
tracks levels   of marine pollution.   For now

I am trying
to quiet   all scenes
in order to feel things   so clearly

the caterpillar can unhook   its clasp
on   ramrod leaf stem   undetected
and the mountains   may at last back off

their strained   remoteness.
Somewhere   a certain snail
will use a pair   of wings

as swim-organs;   interstices
on the bottom   of sea ice
array themselves   as *frail.*

We're most unbrokenly ourselves
when no one is around   to see us.

Still   earlier

today
from a distance of three inches

      I saw another person's face,

   sun-fuzzed
         and rumpled slightly

like a backpack
        dropped

     into the day's exhibit booth.

Because of this
I will cover my eyes in the brine-colored room.
I will say nothing
              for a month of Junes.

What Wittgenstein's College Friend Frank Says

What we can't say, we can't say—and we can't
whistle it either.

Directional Dressed as the Statue of Liberty

The last guy I breeze-dated
        wore a golf shirt tattooed
                with a predator drone.

Silence grew so quiet
           over chicken skewers   you could hear
                  the hiss at the visible

edge of the universe.
                    I secretly hoped he'd lose all strength
           along the left side of his body.

  That wasn't the half of it.

                  The wars within heart's mind:
                to blame for all the wars outside.

Should I have ordered
           Chilean sea bass with corn chorizo
                  ragu?   Why bother to

   look up at sky and find a gap?
                  Which force would you want to thrust
                    off-island first?

            Circle one of these two:

    a.   Calm's mulekick

    b.   Mayhem's edict

              American outbreath
                    smirches the line

        between   cop and soldier,
            soldier and spy,
            spy | | citizen.

     Therefore, riddle with me this lick: *vanishing*
caloric density.

           Stranger yet   the thought

that cells from others sometimes

come to dwell within us: Grandmother cells

contest the place of infants'
in the mother, immortal
jellyfish the while age forward only

to go back and start their lives
once more.

Before the drones
it was as if everyone was young,
said one Pakistani mom.

I have two words for you,
the man's t-shirt intoned
above the aircraft: *Predator Drone.*

Believe anxiety, I reply

to warnings we might slouch
toward its relief.

Some Pakistanis didn't know

what America was before the drones.

I have the ability to almost-hover,

my inner Area 51:

seared earth, chapped lake beds,

zaggy mountain ranges   atop which   only

glowing dung beetles

clump, roll and gallop.

I Jump and Think Like an Endurance Athlete

This British woman,
somewhat high-sprung,

prodded a spot on
her tonsil with a black felt-tip,

tripped in the bath,
then swallowed it—the pen's ink

active even after
two decades' traffic

with stomach acids
in that port

of the abdomen
doctors call *lumen.*

HELLO! said this pen
to an index card

afterward, noting how
rank beauty

sometimes carries the day—
jouk, the no-joke noun

for sudden movement.
On that note, did the traffic

thank you wave
go the way

of the rotary phone? What
time's today's meaning?

Who among us has not once
cried love-wolf? Do you think it's wrong

to have restless legs syndrome?
To really live we should try

and be lifeless too,
as in the first begetting

before pens were born:
Blank sheen. Sounds

clanking around. Then before
you know it the planet's

covered in man and Curiosity
halloos back its results:

*Mars might have sported
living microbes.* We ourselves

are only 1/10th human—
ten microbiota for every cell

in our physiques. I, too, like it
when people call the eye *naked.*

What are *you* looking at?
You bet I'd take it

straight in the ear
from a swan.

Alternative Employment

Q:

A: Mostly I don't. It's perpetual spring for chickens here: Three fair squares in their four-to-a-cage.

Q: A: Size of an album cover. Don't have to worry their heads over predators. Q:

A: They don't mate. They fuss and tussle—stretch and rub, like polyester. We watch them. We walk through, sifting the dead. Most of the hens just cluck and laze. One livewire wants to jump like a galosh on fire. Pecking order. They have it in their cage. Q:

A: Well on the other hand. We put them all out on the floor, it'd take a helluva lot more elbows to gather up eggs. Not to mention they'd cost more. Q:

Q:

Q:

          A: Ma'am, you plan to quit eating eggs sometime this side of the moon?
Q:

A: The chickens will, in pecking order, pick on the weak. Beaks have to go. Chunks of the upper mandibles. Once they taste blood, they keep on going. Cannibals, nearly every one.

Q:

          A. Right you are. Not on your life. Not in a barnyard.

Straight Direction Along a Great Circle

What can I do tonight about the fish farm being run
sub rosa from that 14th-floor apartment?

Or the fact such farms stretch longer than four football fields
and cram over a million fish together in floating pens?

We could begin by looking at the Four Immeasurables.
Or. The nature-based model *adat:*

Islamic-Malay law risen
from pure verb: *to appertain, be proper,* practiced

by the Minangkabau, West Sumatra—
the women there, the *center where fish nets meet;*

spouses or lovers
stay only overnight: a pact tagged

visiting marriage,
each member of the clan

expected to guide—not lead—horizontally, as well
as to enact good *mothership.* Closer

to home, my neighbor who plays bagpipes
snipped his pup's vocal cords. . . .

Oh and how Cicero.
For his candor: head and limbs

lopped off. Maybe living
is mostly for the weak.

Maybe the most we can do
is to leave the world little by little

in order to stay here at all,
waiting to put the goods in the hands of a new clan mother.

Department of Space Studies

Today, this message on the library computer:
The trust relationship between this workstation

and the primary domain failed.
I scratched that

into my *Square Deal*
and kissed the desktop on its left right angle.

Tenderness can take a number
of snap turns, and hell yes

I'm man and girl, two parts
marquee, as well as this sound

of seeing things in your head
but no one fanatically. I'm in a full-time relationship

with the word, and it's mostly good
to lay your riven body in the death position

then just walk away, wonder
how other people are doing

grouped in their secluded skins.
Thus might we finally come to

tongue the aftertaste of some fine blend
of shared umami whose sense of furriness

in the mouth we'd be crazy not to take
to mean full detailed forgiveness

of every anyone—even for giant fuck-ups.
Because why not. Because the space of

the thinkable's so much
larger than the frilled lean-tos

daily dispensed to us. Listen.
The hand purrs

as it fingers the spines
of all the new titles for loan: Take one.

World Upside-Down

Despite the fact I can't lay flat
    two fingers,

on my way home from work
    I walked on my hands

from my corner—
    over grass and elm shadow and across

the sidewalk's light
    upheavals, half the way

to Sunbeam Grocery—fresh blood-chutes
    to the brain with each

stride of the palm,
    pair of inner blue pumps

pretty much off duty;
    spine, lats, and thyroid cartilage elongated fully.

This I do with the soles of my hands:
    cop a feel of the globe

in mega-dimension, how dogs sniff voles
    through fronds of wild rye.

With how much grandeur dandelions keep their minds afloat!
    Noble, with clover laced in

industrial bug juice, Toby a swatch
    of roving cumulus. The whole schmeer,

by which I must now mean the full-on world,
    seems half again as much

a meanness derby as anything else.
    Therefore, let me lay this word in the church of your mouth,

sweet and lanky as a splice of blue grass: *inwit*.
    Sit back, read, and taste this wheat.

Acknowledgements

Sincerest thanks to the editors who first published the following poems, some of which have been revised or recombined since:

Arabesques Review: "*Materfamilias* Leaflet," published under the title "*Materfamilias*";

Best Poem and *Mamas and Papas: On the Sublime and Heartbreaking Art of Parenting:* "Traffic Circle," published under the title "Elations";

Blast Furnace: "Sign Twirler Crunches Some Numbers," under the title "Numbers Ode";

The Cabin: NERVE—Writers in the Attic: "The Hope of Sound," "Straight Direction Along a Great Circle," and "Department of Space Studies";

Cascadia Review: "Rugged Western Individualism, in 3D Display" and "The Three-Body Problem";

Classifieds: An Anthology of Prose Poems: "Enter the Kingdom," "From Staple to Symbol," published under the title "Body Studies," "Junction," published under the title "Old Man," "Of Genders and Genres," and "Intersectional," published under the title "The Couple";

Drafthorse: "Light Wind Lifts Language's Dress Up," published under the title "*Poem xxii* from *Torchie's Book of Days*";

Educe, A Journal of Queer Literature: "Sign Twirler Stands Like Michelangelo's Man in a Circle" and "Sign Twirler Balances Six Rectangles at Once," under the title "Two Poems from *Torchie's Book of Days*";

Fraglit: "Ghost Sign," published under the title "Fight Choreography," and "At the Symposium on the Necessity of Beauty";

Fraglit and *New Poets of the American West:* "Husband";

The Hartskill Review: "A Sign Said *There are 16 Million Eyes in the City,*" published under the title "Poem from *Torchie's Book of Days*";

In Her Place Web Anthology: "Views from a Former Contortionist," published under the title "Hump";

Los Angeles Review: "Garden Variety Glide," published under the title "Garden Variety";

The Meadowland Review: "Sign Twirler Turns the World Upside-Down," under the title "Poem from *Torchie's Book of Days*";

The Mom Egg: "Step on a Crack, You Break," published under the title "Lineage";

OccuPoetry: "Directional Dressed as the Statue of Liberty," published under the title "Poem *xxxiii* from *Torchie's Book of Days*";

Papercuts: "Sign Twirler's Guide to the Multiverse" and "Fifth and State" under the title "Poems from *Torchie's Book of Days*";

Perigee: "Motherhood as Momentary Characteristic";

The Prose-Poem Project: "The Three-Body Problem," "Scrolling Light Box with the Twelve O'clock News," and "The Inner Coat," published under the title "First-Person Triangular";

Roar: "Clean Garage *Rag*";

Shifting Balance Sheets: Women's Stories of Naturalized Citizenship & Cultural Attachment: "Broadsheet from the Family Bed";

Sleet: "Art Must be Useful to the People" and "What Wittgenstein's College Friend Frank Says";

Tawdry Bawdry: "Interspace," published under the title "Revelation";

The Untidy Season: An Anthology of Nebraska Women Poets: "Rugged Western Individualism";

Urban Voices: 51 Poems from 51 American Poets: "Ours is the Age of Pre-Post Hope," published under the title "150 Years of Evenings";

Verse/Chorus: A Call and Response Anthology: "Experiment on Backs of Soup Labels," published under the title "Poem *xix* from *Torchie's Book of Days*";

White Whale Review: "[   ] is a Sign That Means *Hug for the Horse Forequarters of the Hippocampus*," published under the title "[   ]."

The author wishes to thank the editors of *Educe, A Journal of Queer Literature,* for nominating "Sign Twirler Stands Like Michelangelo's Man in a Circle" and "Sign Twirler Balances Six Rectangles at Once" (under different titles) for a Pushcart Prize. The author also extends sincerest thanks to the Boise City Department of Art and History for the honor of serving as Boise Poet Laureate (2013); gratitude also goes out to the Idaho Commission on the Arts for the honor of having served as Idaho Writer-in-Residence (2013-2016), during both of which terms some of these poems were composed.

Books from Etruscan Press

Etruscan Press is Proud of Support Received from

Wilkes University

Youngstown State University

The Ohio Arts Council

The Stephen & Jeryl Oristaglio Foundation

The Nathalie & James Andrews Foundation

The National Endowment for the Arts

The Ruth H. Beecher Foundation

The Bates-Manzano Fund

The New Mexico Community Foundation

Drs. Barbara Brothers & Gratia Murphy Fund

The Rayen Foundation

The Pella Corporation

Founded in 2001 with a generous grant from the Oristaglio Foundation, Etruscan Press is a nonprofit cooperative of poets and writers working to produce and promote books that nurture the dialogue among genres, achieve a distinctive voice, and reshape the literary and cultural histories of which we are a part.

etruscan press
www.etruscanpress.org

Etruscan Press books may be ordered from

Consortium Book Sales and Distribution
800.283.3572
www.cbsd.com

Small Press Distribution
800.869.7553
www.spdbooks.org

Etruscan Press is a 501(c)(3) nonprofit organization.
Contributions to Etruscan Press are tax deductible
as allowed under applicable law.
For more information, a prospectus,
or to order one of our titles,
contact us at books@etruscanpress.org.